AWESOME ANIMALS OF ASIA

The Continent and Its Creatures Great and Small

Nicole K. Orr

The Himalaya Mountains, shown here, are very large and tall. They are in India and Nepal, which are countries in Asia. Mt. Everest is part of the Himalayas, and it's the largest mountain in the world.

Welcome to Asia! Of the world's seven continents, Asia is the largest. Asia is known for its cities and large areas of wilderness.

Asia is bordered by three oceans: the Arctic, Pacific, and Indian oceans. The continent can be divided into six regions. Each of these regions has its own biomes and its own animals.

SIBERIAN TIGER

Length: 12 feet (3.7 meters), including tail
Weight: 700 pounds (318 kilograms)
Habitat: forests of North Asia
Diet: deer, boars, small mammals, and fish

The Siberian (sy-BEER-ee-in) tiger is the largest cat in the world. Despite its name, it does not live in Siberia. Instead, it lives mainly in eastern Russia and northeastern China.

Elk are also called maral (mah-RAAL) in Asia. Males have a loud call that sounds like a bugle, which can be heard very far away. They use this to call out for females.

ELK
Height: 7½ feet (2.3 meters), including antlers
Weight: 600 pounds (272 kilograms)
Habitat: mountains, forests, and grasslands of North and East Asia
Diet: grasses

The Asian elephant is the largest animal in Asia. Elephant trunks are not just for eating. Trunks can also suck up water, then shoot it up into the air so elephants can have a shower. A group of elephants is called a clan.

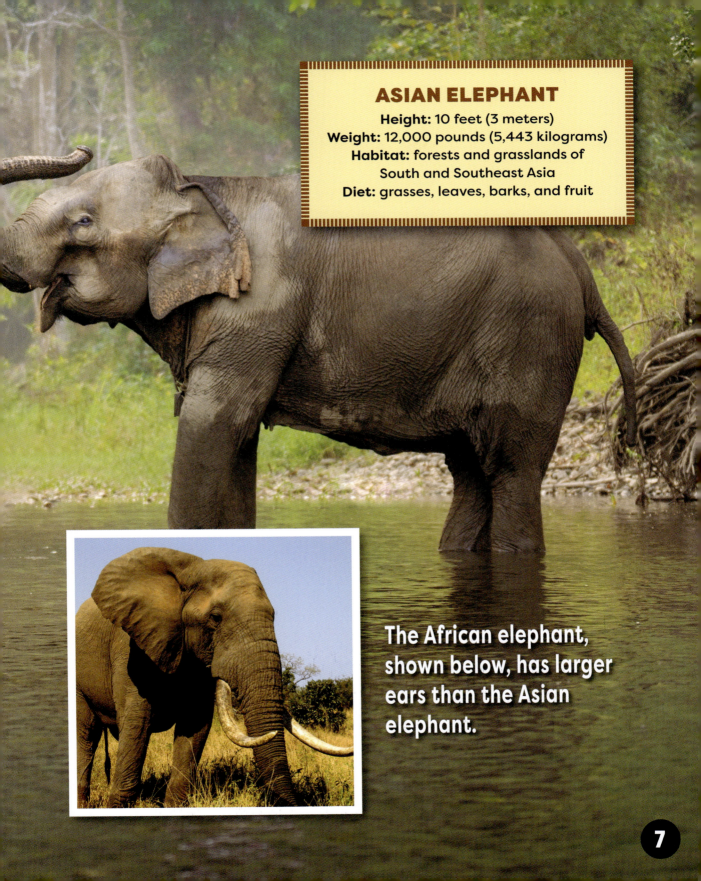

ASIAN ELEPHANT
Height: 10 feet (3 meters)
Weight: 12,000 pounds (5,443 kilograms)
Habitat: forests and grasslands of South and Southeast Asia
Diet: grasses, leaves, barks, and fruit

The African elephant, shown below, has larger ears than the Asian elephant.

GIANT PANDA
Length: 6 feet (1.8 meters)
Weight: 300 pounds (136 kilograms)
Habitat: forests of China
Diet: bamboo

Giant pandas spend most of their day eating or sleeping. They eat mostly bamboo, but it isn't very nutritious, so pandas often seem low on energy.

The Asian black bear has strong arms that are great for climbing trees. It will spend half its day up in a tree. Asian black bears have a V-shaped mark on their chests.

ASIAN BLACK BEAR
Length: 6 feet (1.8 meters)
Weight: 440 pounds (200 kilograms)
Habitat: forests and mountains of East and Southeast Asia
Diet: insects, fruits, honey, and medium-sized mammals

JAPANESE MACAQUE

Height: 22 inches (56 centimeters), not including tail
Weight: 25 pounds (11 kilograms)
Habitat: forests and mountains of Japan
Diet: fruits, leaves, nuts, and insects

The Japanese macaque (**mah-CACK**) is a monkey that likes to live in the cold. When it gets too cold, this macaque will soak in a natural hot spring to warm up. It's the only monkey that makes snowballs!

The tarsier (**TAR-see-er**) can turn its heads all the way around to look behind, and its large eyes help it hunt at night. These small mammals can leap 20 feet (6 meters) in one jump to catch their food.

TARSIER
Height: 6 inches (15.2 centimeters), not including tail
Weight: 3.5 ounces (100 grams)
Habitat: rainforests of Southeast Asia
Diet: insects, lizards, and frogs

Snow leopards are mysterious. They live high in the Himalaya Mountains, and their fur is the perfect camouflage for the rocks and snow around them. It also keeps them warm! For extra warmth, their long fluffy tails can be wrapped around their bodies.

The snow leopard's paw is very large and acts like a snowshoe, helping it walk on top of the snow. A snow leopard can jump 30 feet (9 meters) in one leap.

SNOW LEOPARD

Length: 8 feet (2.4 meters) long, including tail
Weight: 121 pounds (55 kilograms)
Habitat: mountains of South and East Asia
Diet: deer, sheep, and small mammals

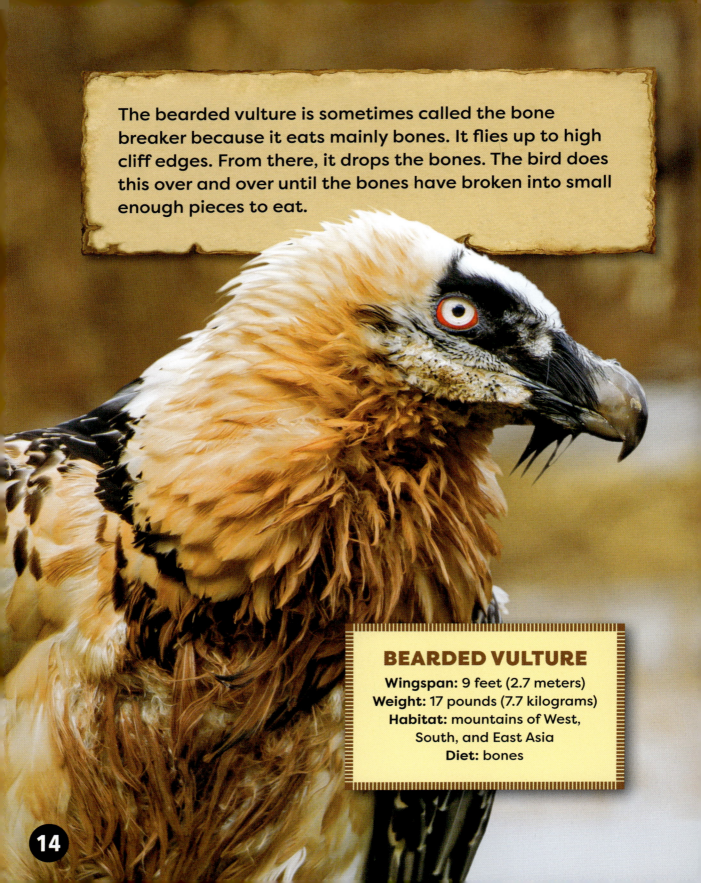

The bearded vulture is sometimes called the bone breaker because it eats mainly bones. It flies up to high cliff edges. From there, it drops the bones. The bird does this over and over until the bones have broken into small enough pieces to eat.

BEARDED VULTURE
Wingspan: 9 feet (2.7 meters)
Weight: 17 pounds (7.7 kilograms)
Habitat: mountains of West, South, and East Asia
Diet: bones

BROWN PRINIA (PRY-NEE-AH)
Length: 6 inches (15 centimeters)
Weight: ½ ounce (14 grams)
Habitat: dry forests of Southeast Asia
Diet: insects

RED-CROWNED CRANE
Height: 5 feet (1.5 meters)
Weight: 18 pounds (8.2 kilograms)
Habitat: wetlands of East Asia
Diet: fish, rodents, grasses, berries, and insects

JAPANESE HONEYBEE

Length: ⅓ inch (1 centimeter)
Habitat: forests and grasslands of Japan
Diet: pollen and nectar

ASIAN GIANT HORNET

Length: 2½ inches (6.4 centimeters)
Habitat: forests of South, Southeast, and East Asia
Diet: insects

The Asian giant hornet can kill more than 40 bees a minute. Giant hornet scouts will release a scent when they find a beehive. The scent calls other hornets to the feast.

Japanese honeybees try to stop these intruders before they release this special scent. They will swarm the Asian giant hornet and wiggle very fast. Wiggling makes the scout hornet so hot it dies.

In warm, dry areas of the Middle East lives the Arabian fat-tailed scorpion. It is sometimes called the man killer because of the deadly venom in its sting.

The Chinese red-headed centipede is also venomous. If a person is bitten, the pain can last for days. Amazingly, people have found safe ways to eat these leggy insects!

ARABIAN FAT-TAILED SCORPION

Length: 4 inches (10.2 centimeters)
Weight: 5.5 grams
Habitat: deserts of West Asia
Diet: insects, spiders, and small lizards

CHINESE RED-HEADED CENTIPEDE

Length: 8 inches (20 centimeters)
Weight: 3 grams
Habitat: forests and grasslands East Asia
Diet: insects and small rodents, snakes, and frogs

ARABIAN ORYX

Height: 4 feet (1.2 meters), not including horns
Weight: 165 pounds (75 kilograms)
Habitat: deserts of West Asia
Diet: grasses, roots, and fruits

The Arabian oryx (**OR-ihx**) has white fur that keeps it cool. It can also survive without drinking water for weeks, like camels. The horn of the Arabian oryx can grow to 5 feet (1.5 meters) long.

Arabian oryxes were once considered extinct in the wild. Extinct means there were no oryxes living in the wild. Only a few were left, all of them in zoos. However, people from around the world made a plan to save the Arabian oryx. Enough oryxes were born to reintroduce them to the wild. This is the first time an animal has come back from being "extinct"!

UROMASTYX

Length: 30 inches (76 centimeters), including tail
Weight: 4½ pounds (2 kilograms)
Habitat: deserts of West Asia
Diet: leaves, vegetables, and seeds

The Uromastyx (yur-oh-MAS-tiks) is also called a spiny-tailed lizard. Its tail is used like a club. It will even stick its tail out of a burrow to warn off predators.

Russell's vipers have a venomous bite. They often appear lazy, but they can lift their entire body off the ground.

RUSSELL'S VIPER

Length: 5 feet (1.5 meters)
Weight: 5 pounds (2.3 kilograms)
Habitat: grasslands of South Asia
Diet: rodents, lizards, crabs, and scorpions

The Komodo (kah-MOH-doh) dragon is the biggest lizard in the world. It lives only on a few islands in Indonesia (in-doh-NEE-ja).

While they typically hide before attacking prey, Komodo dragons can run up to 13 miles (21 kilometers) per hour. That is almost three times faster than the average human jogger.

KOMODO DRAGON

Length: 10 feet (3 meters), including tail
Weight: 300 pounds (136 kilograms)
Habitat: forests and coasts of Indonesia
Diet: water buffalo, pigs, and deer

RED LIONFISH
Length: 18 inches (46 centimeters)
Weight: 2½ pounds (1.2 kilograms)
Habitat: coral reefs of Pacific and Indian Ocean
Diet: fish and crabs

Lionfish are the zebras of the ocean because of their brightly colored stripes. Venom is stored inside each spike on the lionfish's back. Its mouth is large enough to swallow smaller fish in one bite.

The vampire crab looks a little scary. It has a dark blue-purple body and glowing yellow-green eyes. It's nocturnal, meaning it looks for food at night.

VAMPIRE CRAB

Width: 2 inches (5 centimeters)
Weight: ⅓ ounce (10 grams)
Habitat: wetlands in Indonesia
Diet: insects, worms, and plants

ORANGUTAN

Height: 54 inches (137 centimeters)
Weight: 191 pounds (87 kilograms)
Habitat: rainforests of Southeast Asia
Diet: fruits, insects, and leaves

Orangutans' arms are longer than their bodies, which they use to swing from tree to tree. They even make nests in the branches of trees to sleep in.

The orangutan is very smart, finding clever ways to catch or collect food, such as using a stick to direct honey to its mouth. Orangutan children will stay with their mothers for seven or eight years.

The red panda is not related to the giant panda. It is more closely related to weasels and raccoons. However, it does like to eat bamboo. The red panda's fur is used as camouflage with the colorful moss on trees.

Asia is a large place indeed. But many of these animals have very special habitats. With so many people and animals packed into one continent, it's important to share!

RED PANDA

Length: 3½ feet (1.1 meters), including tail
Weight: 17 pounds (7.7 kilograms)
Habitat: mountain forests of South and East Asia
Diet: bamboo, fruits, and insects

FURTHER READING

Books

Allgor, Marie. *Endangered Animals of Asia (Save Earth's Animals!)*. New York: Powerkids Press, 2011.

Kurkov, Lisa. *ASTOUNDING! Asian Animals*. Richmond, Victoria, Australia: Spectrum Publications, 2014.

Murray, Julie. *Komodo Dragons (Asian Animals)*. Edina, MN: Big Buddy Books, 2013.

Spilsbury, Richard, and Louise Spilsbury. *Animals in Danger in Asia*. Portsmouth, NH: Heinemann Publishing, 2013.

Wang, Andrea. *Learning About Asia (Do You Know the Continents?)*. Minneapolis, MN: Lerner Classroom Publications, 2015.

Websites

Active Wild: Asian Animals List with Pictures and Amazing Facts
   https://www.activewild.com/asian-animals

Fun Kids: Top 10 Facts about Asia
   https://www.funkidslive.com/learn/top-10-facts/top-10-facts-about-asia

Ducksters: Asia
   http://www.ducksters.com/geography/asia.php

GLOSSARY

biome (BY-ohm)—Any major region that has a specific climate and supports specific animals and plants.

camouflage (KAM-uh-flahj)—The ability to blend in with the color of the environment.

continent (KON-tih-nunt)—One of the seven great pieces of land on Earth.

extinct (ex-STINKT)—All of a certain type of animal are no longer alive. When an animal can only be found in zoos, it is labeled "extinct in the wild."

population (pop-yuh-LAY-shun)—All of the people in one area, such as a town or country.

prey (PRAY)—An animal that is hunted for food.

wilderness (WIL-der-nis)—An area that has not been disturbed by people.

venom (VEN-um)—Poison inserted into the body instead of eaten.

PHOTO CREDITS

Inside front cover—Shutterstock/ruboart; p. 1—Flickr/Soren Wolf; p. 2 (Asia map)—Shutterstock/Peter Hermes Furian; p. 2 (world map)—Shutterstock/Maxger; pp. 2-3—Shutterstock/Prawat Thananithaporn; pp. 4-5—Mathias Appel; p. 5 (elk)—Shutterstock/Galyna Andrushko; pp. 6-7—Shutterstock/Nuamfolio; p. 6 (inset)—Shutterstock/Robby Holmwood; pp. 8-9—Shutterstock/Wonderly Imaging; p. 9 (black bear)—Shutterstock/Somchai Siriwanarangson; pp. 10-11—Shutterstock/Pises Tungittipokai; p. 10 (inset)—Shutterstock/slowmotiongli; p. 11 (tarsier)—Flickr/Jan Hazevoet; p. 12 (inset)—Shutterstock/Chris Desborough; pp. 12-13—Shutterstock/Jim Cumming; pp. 14-15 (crane)—Shutterstock/Ondrej Prosicky; p. 14 (vulture)—Flickr/Tambako the Jaguar; p. 15 (prinia)—Artemy Voishansky; p. 16 (honeybee)—Shutterstock/Dave Hansche; pp. 16-17—Shutterstock/Panga Media; p. 17 (scorpion)—Shutterstock/Ernie Cooper; pp. 18-19—Shutterstock/Nimit Virdi; pp. 20-21—Eitan F.; pp. 22-23—Flickr/Poppet Maulding; p. 25 (crab)—Shutterstock/Lauren Suryanata; pp. 26-27—Shutterstock/Rita Enes; p. 27 (inset)—Flickr/Chem 7; p. 28 (inset)—Shutterstock/Lukas Zdrazil; pp. 28-29—Mathias Appel; inside back cover—Shutterstock/ruboart.

All other photos—Public Domain. Every measure has been taken to find all copyright holders of material used in this book. In the event any mistakes or omissions have happened within, attempts to correct them will be made in future editions of the book.

CHECK OUT THE OTHER BOOKS IN THE AWESOME ANIMALS SERIES

Awesome Animals of Africa
Awesome Animals of Antarctica
Awesome Animals of Australia
Awesome Animals of Europe and the United Kingdom
Awesome Animals of North America
Awesome Animals of South America

© 2024 by Curious Fox Books™, an imprint of Fox Chapel Publishing Company, Inc., 903 Square Street, Mount Joy, PA 17552.

Awesome Animals of Asia is a revision of *The Animals of Asia*, published in 2017 by Purple Toad Publishing, Inc. Reproduction of its contents is strictly prohibited without written permission from the rights holder.

Paperback ISBN 979-8-89094-099-5
Hardcover ISBN 979-8-89094-100-8

Library of Congress Control Number: 2024933039

To learn more about the other great books from Fox Chapel Publishing, or to find a retailer near you, call toll-free 800-457-9112 or visit us at *www.FoxChapelPublishing.com*.

We are always looking for talented authors. To submit an idea, please send a brief inquiry to acquisitions@foxchapelpublishing.com.

Fox Chapel Publishing makes every effort to use environmentally friendly paper for printing.

Printed in Malaysia